**Please check all items for damages
before leaving the Library.
Thereafter you will be held
responsible for all injuries
to items beyond reasonable wear.**

Helen M. Plum Memorial Library

Lombard, Illinois

A daily fine will be charged for
overdue materials.

FEB 2011

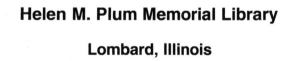

To Ellie, Jireh, and Nathan—
I hope you always find humor in learning

Special thanks to Mrs. Jeanne Gibson at Lyman High School—
Thank you for all you have done and continue to do for your students.
You truly do make a difference!
—T. S.

For Louisa, fearless tamer of mathfacts and cows
—T. M.

Text Copyright © 2010 Taryn Souders
Illustration Copyright © 2010 Tatjana Mai-Wyss

Sleeping Bear Press™

315 E. Eisenhower Parkway, Ste. 200
Ann Arbor, MI 48108
www.sleepingbearpress.com

© 2010 Sleeping Bear Press is an imprint of Gale,
a part of Cengage Learning.

Printed and bound in China.

First Edition

10 9 8 7 6 5 4 3 2 1

Library of Congress Cataloging-in-Publication Data

Souders, Taryn, 1977-
Whole-y cow!: fractions are fun / written by Taryn Souders;
illustrated by Tatjana Mai-Wyss.
p. cm.
ISBN 978-1-58536-460-2
1. Fractions—Juvenile literature. 2. Mathematics—Juvenile poetry.
I. Mai-Wyss, Tatjana, 1972- ill. II. Title.
QA117.S68 2010
513.2'6—dc22

Whole-y Cow!
Fractions Are Fun

Written by **Taryn Souders**

Illustrated by **Tatjana Mai-Wyss**

One whole cow was calmly eating hay,

and decided to act differently
on this particular day.

One whole cow what should she do?

4

Moo while her friends paint one half blue!

What fraction of the cow is blue?
What fraction of the cow is white?

One whole cow
patriotic through and through,
wore a swimsuit
that was red, white, and blue.

6

What fraction of the swimsuit is red?
What fraction of the swimsuit is white?
What fraction of the swimsuit is blue?

One whole cow
was eating ice cream,

8

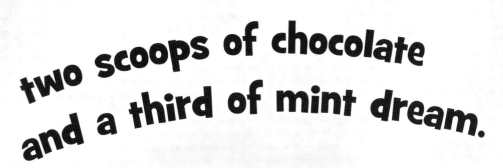

two scoops of chocolate
and a third of mint dream.

What fraction of the ice cream is chocolate?
What fraction of the ice cream is mint dream?

One whole cow balanced on a peg,

got a little klutzy and hurt one leg.

What fraction of the legs is hurt?
What fraction of the legs is not hurt?

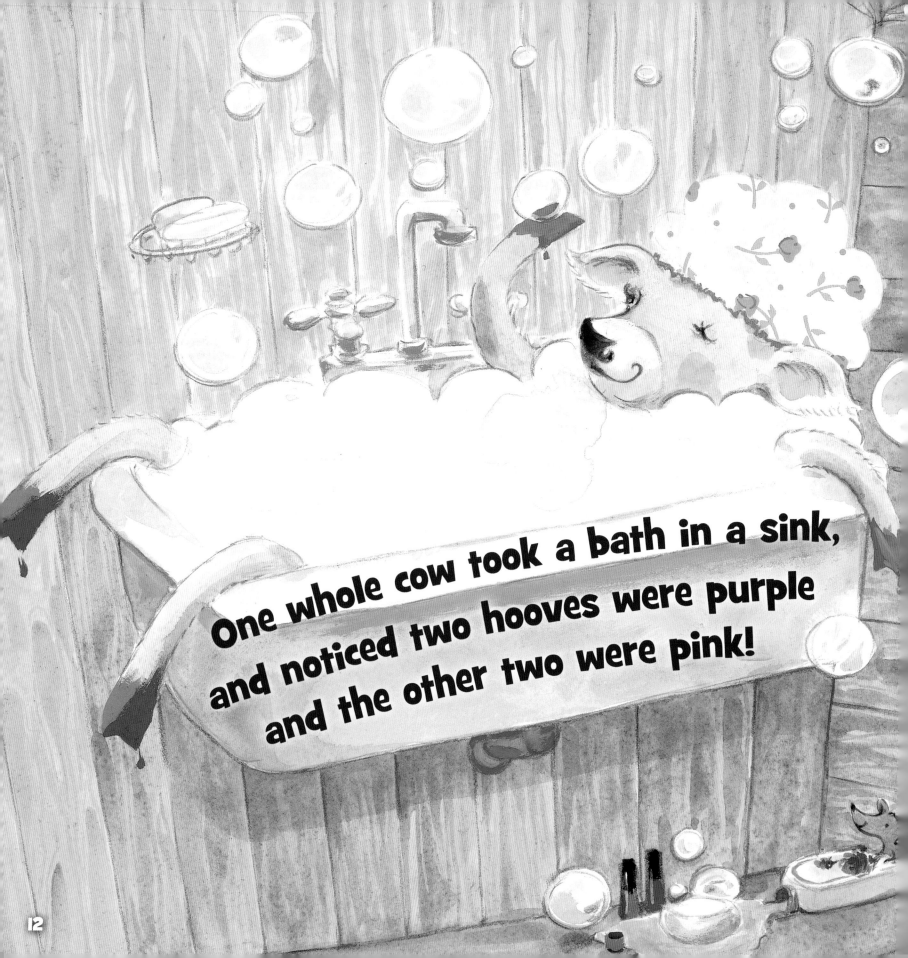

One whole cow took a bath in a sink,
and noticed two hooves were purple
and the other two were pink!

What fraction of the hooves is purple?
What fraction of the hooves is pink?

One whole cow sat down to play the cello,
while eating a daisy
that was orange and bright yellow.

14

What fraction of the daisy's petals is yellow?

What fraction of the daisy's petals is orange?

One whole cow had a fish named Fred,

who painted six spots on the cow's back red!

What fraction of the spots is red?
What fraction of the spots is blue?

One whole cow who danced with such grace, entered a contest and won first place.

What fraction of the ribbons is blue?

What fraction of the ribbons is red?

What fraction of the ribbons is yellow?

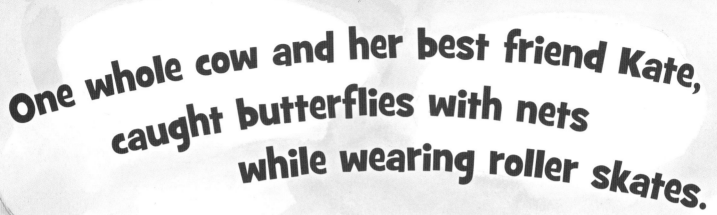

One whole cow and her best friend Kate,
caught butterflies with nets
while wearing roller skates.

What fraction of the cow's butterflies is blue?
What fraction of Kate's butterflies is red?
What fraction of the total butterflies caught is purple?

One whole cow was calmly eating hay,

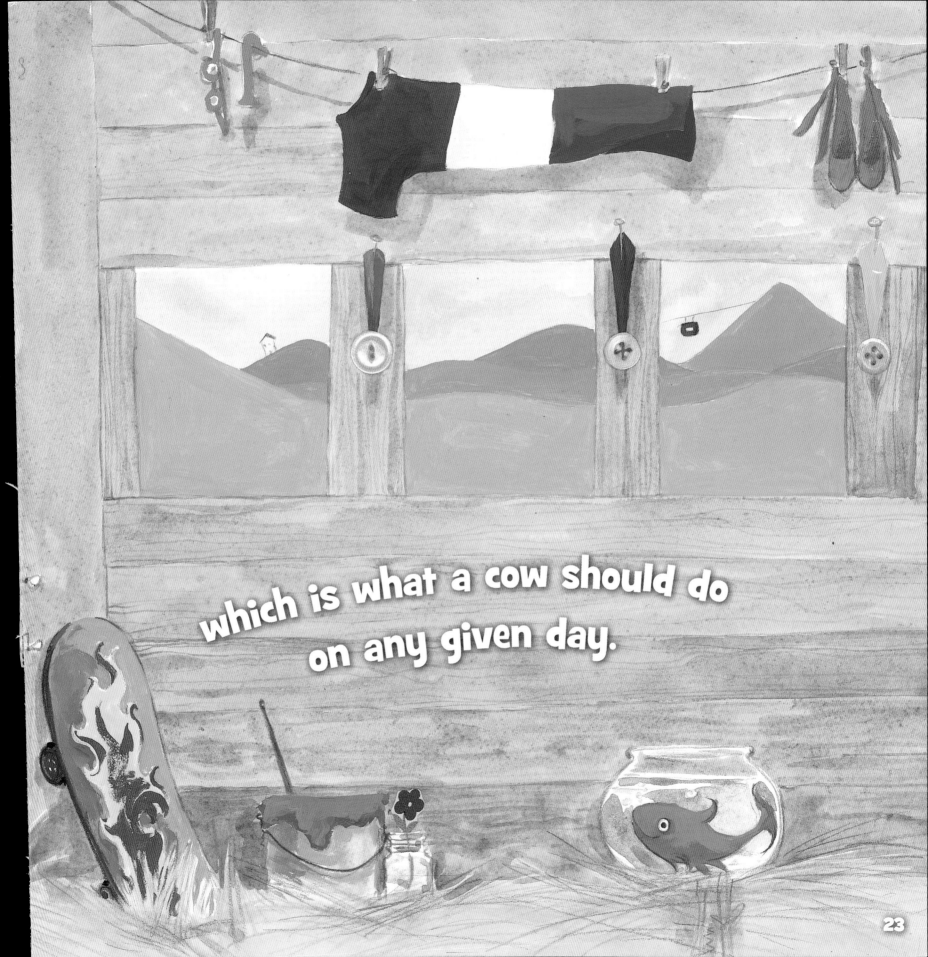

which is what a cow should do
on any given day.

What fraction of the cow is blue?
  Answer: ½
What fraction of the cow is white?
  Answer: ½

Pages 4-5

What fraction of the swimsuit is red?
  Answer: ⅓
What fraction of the swimsuit is white?
  Answer: ⅓
What fraction of the swimsuit is blue?
  Answer: ⅓

Pages 6-7

What fraction of the ice cream is chocolate?
  Answer: ⅔
What fraction of the ice cream is mint dream?
  Answer: ⅓

Pages 8-9

What fraction of the legs is hurt?
  Answer: ¼
What fraction of the legs is not hurt?
  Answer: ¾

Pages 10-11

What fraction of the hooves is purple?
  Answer: ²/₄ (Reduces to ½)
What fraction of the hooves is pink?
  Answer: ²/₄ (Reduces to ½)

Pages 12-13

What fraction of the daisy's petals is yellow?
    Answer: ²⁄₅
What fraction of the daisy's petals is orange?
    Answer: ³⁄₅

What fraction of the spots is red?
    Answer: ⁶⁄₈ (Reduces to ³⁄₄)
What fraction of the spots is blue?
    Answer: ²⁄₈ (Reduces to ¹⁄₄)

Pages 14–15

Pages 16–17

What fraction of the ribbons is blue?
    Answer: ¹⁄₃
What fraction of the ribbons is red?
    Answer: ¹⁄₃
What fraction of the ribbons is yellow?
    Answer: ¹⁄₃

Pages 18–19

What fraction of the cow's butterflies is blue?
    Answer: ²⁄₄ (Reduces to ¹⁄₂)
What fraction of Kate's butterflies is red?
    Answer: ⁴⁄₆ (Reduces to ²⁄₃)
What fraction of the total butterflies caught is purple?
    Answer: ⁴⁄₁₀ (Reduces to ²⁄₅)

Pages 20–21